A Fun Guide just ♥ for Girls ages 6~9

Just For Me!
The Bible

Katrina Cassel

LEGACY PRESS®
www.LegacyExpress.com

Dedication:

To the little ones -- Jasmine, Kayla, and Phoenix.

May God's Word be the Light that guides your way through life.

A special thanks to:

Rick : Best friend and guide

Tyler: Firstborn

Jessica: Firstborn princess

Adam: Warrior in the making

Jasmine: My joy and song

Teresa who, as always, was ready with suggestions

The Legacy Press team who puts it all together

JUST FOR ME: THE BIBLE

©2010 by Legacy Press, fifth printing

ISBN 10: 1-58411-083-X

ISBN 13: 978-1-58411-083-5

Legacy reorder#: LP48412

JUVENILE NONFICTION / Religion / Christianity / Christian Life

Legacy Press

P.O. Box 261129

San Diego, CA 92196

www.LegacyExpress.com

Mixed Sources

Product group from well-managed forests and other controlled sources

www.fsc.org   Cert no. GFA-COC-001990

©1996 Forest Stewardship Council

FSC

Cover Illustrator: Dave Carleson

Interior Illustrator: Shelley Dieterichs

Scriptures are from the *Holy Bible: New International Version* (North American Edition), ©1973, 1978, 1984 by the International Bible Society. Used by permission of Zondervan Bible Publishers.

Printed in the United States of America

Table of Contents

Hi Girlfriend! ◄......

Welcome to *Just For Me: The Bible!*

The Bible is an awesome book. But it's more than just a book; it's God's Word to us. The Bible tells about how

God made the world, how we (and that means YOU!) are His most precious creations, and how to live in a way that is pleasing to Him. It tells about heroes and bad people, kings and queens, shepherds and sheep, and more (did I mention a huge flood and millions of frogs?)

Throughout *Just for Me: The Bible* you'll read about two girls, Katie and Sarah, who are probably much like you. In addition to the stories about Katie and Sarah, there are crafts, puzzles, and activities that will help you learn about the Bible in fun ways. I hope you'll come along for the adventure — and bring a friend.

Let's get started!

What is the Bible?

Chapter 1

Tales from
Sarah & Katie

Katie walked down the aisles of books in the library. There was row after row of different kinds of books. She wasn't sure what she wanted to read.

"Wow, this is great," she said to her sister Sarah. "I'm sure glad they opened this library branch near us."

"Me too," Sarah agreed. "I can't wait to see what they have in the mystery section."

"I think I'll get some animal books," Katie said.

Later at home, Katie and Sarah sat down to read the books they'd checked out.

"Looks like you found a lot of books you liked at the new library," Dad said when he arrived home from work.

"We did," Sarah said. "I got two mysteries and two biographies."

"And I checked out three animal books," Katie said.

"You know, that reminds me of another library," Dad said. "A library we each have. Can you guess what it is?"

"Hmmm. I have a lot of books," Katie said, "but not enough to be a library."

"Me either," Sarah said.

"I'll give you more clues," Dad said. "This library has sixty-six books in it. It has books about good people and bad people, books about friends and families, books about the only perfect person ever to live, and books about how we should live."

"I got it," Katie said. "You're talking about the Bible."

"Right," Dad agreed.

"I never thought of the Bible as a library," Sarah said.

"It's a library made up of sixty-six different books divided into two big parts — The Old Testament and The New Testament," Dad replied.

"And those parts are divided into books," Katie said. "I learned that at church club. The Old Testament has 39 books and the New Testament has 27 books."

"Exactly right," Dad agreed. "Do you know how we got the Bible?"

"From God?" Sarah guessed.

"Yes, from God. But He used about forty men to help Him and it took around 1,500 years to write the whole Bible. Here's how it happened," Dad said.

How We Got Our Bible

Because of His love for us, God wanted to teach us about Himself, Jesus, and the Holy Spirit. He knew which stories and people would show us what we need to know to live in a way that pleases Him.

God told these people what he wanted written. They knew in their hearts what message God wanted them to write. They used their own words to tell God's message and He made sure they didn't make any mistakes. They often wrote on papyrus, a kind of paper made from

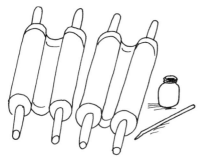

reeds grown in Egypt, or on dried animal skins. These were rolled up into scrolls. These men didn't all live at the same time. Some lived back when Abraham did and others lived over a thousand years later when Jesus lived.

Over the years, scribes carefully copied the

scriptures onto new scrolls.
Later, the words were written
by hand into books. Around
1440 A.D. the printing press
was invented and Bibles could
be made much faster.

Now Bibles come in all colors and sizes. Some Bibles
are written for adults and some are written for kids just
like you.

Why is the Bible so important?

The Bible is the only book that God wrote. It's His
message to us. In the Bible, God tells us:

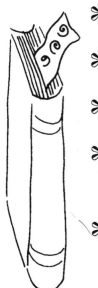

❋ How the world began

❋ What God is like

❋ How sin started

❋ What happened to people who
obeyed God

❋ What happened to people who
disobeyed God

✱ How Jesus was born

✱ Why Jesus had to die

✱ What happened to the first people who believed in Jesus

✱ How God wants you to live

✱ And a whole lot more!

WoW! The Bible sounds like a book full of information and adventures. There's a lot to learn! Let's start at the beginning. But first, here is a bookmark you can make to keep in your Bible while you learn about God's Word.

Make It!

❂ Bible Bookmark ❂

We've learned that God wrote the Bible. God didn't use a pencil to write the Bible, but this pencil bookmark can remind you that God is the author of the Bible.

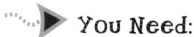

▶ You Need:

You can use colored paper in place of the craft foam.

✱ Pink craft foam 1½ inches by 2 inches

Yellow craft foam 7 inches by 2 inches

 Tan craft foam about 2 inches by 2 inches

 Piece of poster board 2 inches wide by 8 inches long

 Scissors

 Glue

 Black marker

 Two 2 inch pieces of gold ribbon or curl tie

 Ruler

 To Do:

 Cut 1½ inches at the end of the poster board to look like the sharp tip of a pencil.

 Glue the pink foam at the square end of the poster board to look like the pencil eraser.

Glue the yellow foam the length of the poster board so that it touches the eraser.

Cut the tan craft foam to cover the tip of the pencil and glue to the poster board.

11

❋ Glue one piece of gold ribbon where the yellow and pink come together.

❋ Glue one piece of gold ribbon where the yellow and tan come together.

❋ Allow this to dry.

❋ Use the black marker to make the lead pencil point.

❋ Write, *"All Scripture is God-breathed"* — 2 Timothy 3:16 on the bookmark.

❋ Allow it to dry thoroughly, then put it in your Bible.

How It All Began

Tales from
Sarah
& Katie

"Hey," Katie said to Sarah. "How did you get to the end of your book so quickly?"

"I didn't. I just couldn't wait to find out how it ended!" Sarah said.

"You read the end of the mystery first? That's cheating. And it won't be as much fun when you read the book. You'll know what's going to happen," Katie said.

"I know. But I just had to read the ending," Sarah said. She flipped back to chapter two where she was reading.

How it All Began

Sarah may have spoiled the mystery by reading the ending first, but you can read the Bible in any order. For this book, let's start at the beginning. The first five books are called the books of Law. Moses wrote these five books.

Genesis is a book of beginnings. In it you can read about the beginning of:

✳ The world (Genesis 1)

✳ People and animals (Genesis 1-2)

✳ Sin (Genesis 3)

* God's promise of salvation (Genesis 3)

* Rainbows (Genesis 9)

* Different languages (Genesis 11)

* The Israelite people—God's chosen people
  (Genesis 12)

God Creates the World (Genesis 1)

Before God created the world, there was nothing. No color, no shapes, no light, no life. Then God spoke and the world was created. What did He create each day? Use the code to find out.

> A=1, B=2, D=3, E=4, F=5, G=6, H=7, I=8, K=9, L=10
> M=11, N=12, O=13, P=14, R=15, S=16, T=17, U=18, Y=19

Day One: _D_ _A_ _Y_ and _N_ _I_ _G_ _H_ _T_
         3   1   19   12 8 6 7 17

Day Two: ___ ___ ___ and ___ ___ ___
        16 4 1   16 9 19

Day Three: ___ ___ ___ ___ ,
         10 1 12 3

___ ___ ___ ___ ___ ___ and ___ ___ ___ ___ ___
14 10 1 12 17 16   17 15 4 4 16

Day Four: ___ ___ ___, ___ ___ ___ ___
          16   18   12   11   13   13   12

and ___ ___ ___ ___ ___
    16   17   1   15   16

Day Five: ___ ___ ___ ___ ___ and ___ ___ ___ ___
        2   8   15   3   16   5   8   16   7

Day Six: ___ ___ ___ ___ ___ ___ ___
       1   12   8   11   1   10   16

and ___ ___ ___
    11   1   12

Day Seven: ___ ___ ___ ___ ___ ___ ___ ___ ___
        6   13   3   15   4   16   17   4   3

The first man that God created was named Adam. God knew that Adam would be lonely, so God created Eve to keep Adam company. They lived in a beautiful garden called Eden. All of the animals lived in the garden too. God told Adam he could eat any of the fruit he wanted except for the fruit from one special tree.

One day Satan, disguised as a serpent, found Eve in the garden. He told her, "You should eat that good fruit. When you eat it you will be like God." Eve took some of the fruit from the forbidden tree and ate it. Then she gave some to Adam and he ate it too.

Adam and Eve knew they had disobeyed when they ate the fruit. This was the beginning of sin. They hid from God. But God knew what they had done. He was sad they had disobeyed. Because of this disobedience, everyone is born a sinner and needs a Savior. But God already had a plan. One day He would send Jesus to be the Savior of the world.

Eve had trouble obeying God's rules. Do you obey the rules at school and home?

Write one rule that you are going to try hard to keep: _____

_____

_____

_____

_____

_____

A Fresh Start

After the first sin in the Garden of Eden, things got worse. Adam and Eve's son Cain killed his brother Abel out of anger and jealousy. People lied and cheated. The world kept getting more and more sinful. Finally God decided to destroy the earth and start over with one family. Do you know whose family that was?

Right! Noah's family. Noah was the only person who was living in a way that pleased God.

Noah's Floating Zoo (Genesis 6-9)

God told Noah to build a boat. There were no hardware stores where Noah could buy wood and tools. He had to do everything himself. It took him 120 years to build the ark (people lived a lot longer back then). It had to be big enough to hold Noah, his family, and lots of animals.

Once Noah finished the ark and everyone was safely inside, God sent rain for forty days and nights. It destroyed everything. Even after it stopped raining, it was a long time before the land was dry enough for the people and animals to get off of the ark.

Noah's family and all the critters were very happy to finally be off the big boat. The world didn't look like it had before. New grass and plants were just starting to grow again. Noah, his family, and all the animals would have to find or build new homes.

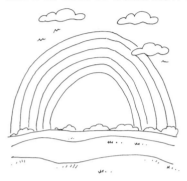

God put a beautiful rainbow in the sky as a promise that He would never again destroy the world with a flood.

Do You Know?

God wanted the pairs of animals to have babies and refill the world with animals. Do you know what different animal babies are called? Draw a line to match the animal name on the left with the baby name on the right.

Lion	Hatchling
Cat	Cub
Horse	PIGLET
KANGAROO	Foal
Alligator	Kitten
Pig	Joey

Tales from
Sarah
& Katie

Katie looked around her room. It was a mess!

"Sarah, can you help me? " she asked. "My stuff is all over the place."

"I'm excited about moving," Katie said, packing her things in a box. "But I'm nervous about starting a new school."

"Me, too. But at least we know where we are going," Sarah said. "Remember our Sunday school lesson about Abraham? Abraham was a faithful man who God had blessed with a loving wife and many riches. God told him to pack up and move without even telling him where he was going."

When Katie and Sarah were done packing, they made special signs for their bedroom doorknobs at their new house. You can make one too.

Make It!

❁ Doorknob Hanger ❁

This craft will look great on your bedroom doorknob. If you have brothers or sisters, they may want to make one also. Every time you see it, you can think about Abraham and his family. Their story is next.

 ## You Need:

✳ Foam board or poster board cut to a doorknob hanger shape or a precut doorknob hanger from a craft store

✳ Things to decorate the board — foam letters, foam pieces such as butterflies, rainbows, etc. Colored pencils or markers also work well if you are making this project with poster board.

✳ Glue

✳ Scissors

 ## To Do:

✳ Use foam letters or markers to write a message such as "Katie's Room" (use your own name) or "My Room." Arrange the letters on your doorknob

21

hanger to make sure the message fits. Then glue the letters one at a time to the doorknob hanger. If you are using poster board and pencils or markers, carefully letter the message on your doorknob hanger. Let it dry.

✽ Decorate it using foam pieces or by drawing pictures on the doorknob hanger.

✽ Let it dry if needed, then hang it on your bedroom doorknob.

Abraham's Moving Day (Genesis 12)

God told Abraham to leave his home in Ur and go to the land of Canaan. Abraham and his wife Sarah packed their belongings (their names were Abram and Sarai at the time of their move.) They prepared the family and animals for the move. It was a slow trip because they used camels to carry their

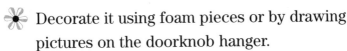

belongings and camels don't go very fast. Abraham also had to follow the river to have water for all of his animals. That made the trip much longer.

God wanted Abraham to be the leader of a great nation. He made a covenant with Abraham. This means he made a special promise to Abraham. God promised to make Abraham a great nation. He promised to bless him his whole life. He promised to make Abraham's name great and to give Abraham's family the land of Canaan.

When God made these promises, Abraham and Sarah didn't have any children yet and they wondered how God would keep His promises. But when Abraham was 100 and Sarah was 90, they had a son they named Isaac. Abraham and Sarah were happy to finally have a child.

Abraham is Faithful (Genesis 22)

Have you ever had to do something that was hard? Maybe this was something you didn't want to do. Maybe you had to share your favorite toy. Or give your sister part of your treat. Maybe you had to give up going to a birthday party or your favorite park. Well, God asked Abraham to do something harder than any of those things! Use the pictures below to tell the story of Abraham and Isaac.

| Abraham | Isaac | Donkey | Lamb | Ram |

One day God spoke to . He said, "Take your only son, , whom you love and go into the wilderness.

Sacrifice 😊 there as a burnt offering."

Usually 🧔 would sacrifice a 🐑 to God. Why would God ask him to give up his only son? 🧔 was sad, but he knew he must obey God. The next morning 🧔 loaded up his 🐴 and headed out with 😊 .

😊 asked his father, "Where is the 🐑 we are going to sacrifice?"

"God will provide the sacrifice," 🧔 said.

As 🧔 was preparing to sacrifice 😊 , God spoke from heaven. He said, "Now I know you are willing to obey Me even if it means giving up your only son."

🧔 saw a 🐏 caught in the bushes and sacrificed it to God.

Do You Know? What character trait does the Bible say Abraham had? Color each space that has a dot in it to find out.

Joseph

When Isaac was grown he married a woman named Rebekah. They had twin boys named Jacob and Esau.

Jacob grew up and fell in love with a woman named Rachel. Rachel's father tricked Jacob into marrying Leah, Rachel's older sister instead. Jacob still loved Rachel, so he married her too. (You could have more than one wife back then.) Jacob always loved Rachel the most. Out of all his sons, Jacob loved Joseph best because Joseph was the first son born to Rachel.

Joseph's brothers hated him because he was the favorite. They sold him as a slave and told their father that a wild animal had killed him! Joseph was taken to Egypt. Joseph was wise and soon he was in charge of

25

many things. Then something bad happened. He was put into prison for something he didn't do.

Everyone forgot about Joseph until one day when the pharaoh had a dream. No one could tell him what it meant. Then someone remembered that Joseph (with God's help) could tell what dreams meant.

The pharaoh told Joseph his dream. God showed Joseph that the pharaoh's dream meant that there would be seven years with lots of food. Then there would be seven years with no food. The pharaoh put Joseph in charge of saving up enough food during the first seven years to feed everyone during the second seven years when no food would grow.

Joseph's Brothers

During the seven years when nothing grew, Joseph's brothers ran out of food. They visited the palace where Joseph was in charge so they could buy food. Joseph recognized them but they didn't know who Joseph was. He had grown into a man.

Joseph forgave his brothers for selling him as a slave. He told them, "You tried to harm me but God used it for good. He used me to save the people from famine."

Joseph's brothers went back to their homeland and returned with their father. They all lived with Joseph in Egypt.

Forgiving Others

It's not easy to forgive others when they do something wrong to you. God helped Joseph forgive his brothers. What does the Bible say about forgiveness?

Cross out all the x's below. Write the rest of the letters in order on the line.

F x o r x g i v x e a x x s t h x e x L o x r d x x f x o r g x a v x e y o x u.

——— —— —— —— —— —— ——   —— ——

—— —— —— —— —— ——

—— —— —— —— —— —— ——   —— —— ——.

— Colossians 3:12

Exodus tells of the Israelites' exit from Egypt.

Joseph's brothers and all their wives and children moved to Egypt to be with Joseph. Many years passed. Now there were over two million of God's special people, the Israelites, living in Egypt. The king thought the

Israelites might form an army and fight against the Egyptian people. He decided to make the Israelites his

slaves to keep that from happening. He made them do hard work all day in the sun.

No matter how hard the king made the Israelites work, there were more and more of them. The king was worried. "Throw all the baby boys into the Nile River," he ordered.

Moses' Floating Bed (Exodus 2)

Moses was one of the baby boys who the king wanted to harm. Read the following rebus story to learn about baby Moses.

Baby

Basket

Princess

One day Jochebed had a . Jochebed loved her

 . At first, she hid him in her house and made sure

he stayed very quiet. Then Jochebed made a plan to save

her 👶 . Jochebed made a floating 🧺 and waterproofed it. She put her 👶 in the 🧺 and hid it among the bulrushes at the river's edge.

Moses' sister Miriam hid nearby watching the 🧺 . The 🧺 floated near the 👳 who was bathing in the river. The 👳 found 👶 Moses. She wanted to keep him for her own. The 👳 called him "Moses" meaning "I drew him out of the water."

Miriam ran out from her hiding place. "Would you like someone to care for your 👶 ?" she asked the 👳 . Moses' own mother cared for him until he was old enough to live at the palace with the 👳 . Even though Moses was living in an Egyptian palace and not with his own family, God never stopped watching over him. And Moses always loved God.

God Calls Moses (Exodus 3)

One day God asked Moses to do a special job. He wanted Moses to tell the pharaoh to free the Israelite slaves. Moses saw a bush on fire but the bush wasn't burned by the fire. He went closer and heard a voice

say, "Take off your shoes. You are on holy ground."

God was speaking to Moses. He told him "Go to Pharaoh and tell him to let My people go."

Moses asked his brother Aaron to go with him to talk to the pharaoh. They spoke to Pharaoh many times, but each time he refused to let the Israelite slaves go free.

Tales from
Sarah
Katie

Katie and Sarah were helping their dad set up the tent. The family was camping in the woods by a lake. They had been working hard preparing for their move and were ready for a fun break together.

"I like camping," Katie said. "But I hate all these mosquitoes!"

"Me too," Sarah agreed. "Camping would be more fun without the bugs!"

"If you don't like bugs and mosquitoes, can you imagine what it would have been like to live through the ten plagues?" their dad asked.

"No thank you," Sarah said. "All those gnats and grasshoppers? Not for me."

"Not for me either," Katie said. "I can't imagine frogs and flies everywhere!"

The Ten Bad Things (Exodus 7-12)

Because Pharaoh refused to free the Israelites, God sent ten terrible plagues to Egypt.

❋ God turned the water in the Nile River to blood. All the fish died and the people didn't have any water.

❋ God sent loads of frogs to cover the whole country.

❋ God turned all the dust of the ground into gnats.

❋ God filled up all the houses and land with flies.

❋ God caused all the Egyptian's livestock to die — cattle, donkeys, horses, camels, sheep, and goats.

✳ God caused horrible sores to break out on the Egyptians' skin.

✳ God sent hail that killed all the unprotected animals, people, and crops.

✳ God sent locusts to eat all the crops and trees left after the hailstorm.

✳ God made it totally dark for three days.

✳ God caused the first born of all the people and animals to die—but He saved the faithful Israelites.

Finally the Pharaoh decided to let the people go. There was great excitement among the Israelites as they gathered their families and belongings and started a long line out of Egypt.

Tales from
Sarah & Katie

Katie and Sarah had all their things packed for their move. Now it was finally time to load the truck.

"Mom," Katie asked. "Can we take snacks with us?"

"Please, Mom? It might take a long time to unload the truck and we'll be hungry," Sarah said.

"Okay," Mom agreed. "We'll make a special travel snack. Let's look in the kitchen and see what hasn't been packed yet."

Katie and Sarah followed their mom to the kitchen. They made a special travel snack. You can make it too, even if you aren't traveling. It's easy to make and not messy to eat in the car.

Katie and Sarah's Travel Snack

Make It!

 **You Need:**

* Large zip sealed bag

* Two cups of unsweetened cereal such as Chex® or Cheerios®

* ½ cup of M&Ms® or other chocolate bits

* ½ cup of pretzels

* ½ cup of raisins

* ½ cup of miniature marshmallows

 To Do:

* Pour all the ingredients into the zip sealed bag.

* Fasten the bag and shake.

* Enjoy!

The People Complain (Exodus 17)

God led the people out of Egypt and protected them but it wasn't long before they began to complain. The water tasted bad and they were hungry. God heard the people and promised to give them all that they needed. He sent manna for them to eat, but they still complained.

One day the people stopped at a place where there was no water to drink. "Why did you bring us here to die of thirst? We were better off as slaves," they said. "At least then we had food to eat and water to drink." The people were so mad at Moses that they picked up stones to throw at him!

Do You Know? What did God tell Moses

about getting water for the people? Look at the two letters below the first line. What letter comes between them? Write it on the line. This will reveal God's instructions to Moses.

___ ___ ___ ___ ___ ___   ___ ___ ___
rt   su   qs   hj   jl   df   su   gi   df

___ ___ ___ ___ ,   ___ ___ ___
qs   np   bd   jl   zb   mo   ce

34

___ ___ ___ ___ ___   ___ ___ ___ ___

vx   zb   su   df   qs   vx   hj   km   km

___ ___ ___ ___   ___ ___ ___

bd   np   ln   df   np   tv   su

___ ___   ___ ___   ___ ___ ___

np   eg   hj   su   eg   np   qs

___ ___ ___   ___ ___ ___ ___ ___ ___

su   gi   df   oq   df   np   oq   km   df

___ ___   ___ ___ ___ ___ ___.

su   np   ce   qs   hj   mo   jl

— Exodus 17:6

The Ten Commandments (Exodus 19-20)

God had some special rules He wanted His people to follow. They were called The Ten Commandments. God wrote them down on two stone tablets. The first four rules talk about how you are to treat God.

1. Let God be more important to you than anything else.

2. Don't worship anything but God.

3. Don't use God's name in a wrong way.

4. Set aside one day of the week to worship God in special ways.

The next six rules are about how we are to treat others.

5. Respect your parents.

6. Don't kill anyone.

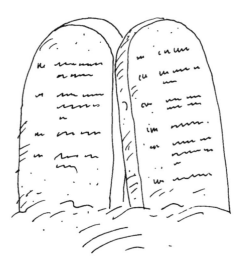

7. Once you are married, save your love for your husband or wife.

8. Don't take anything that isn't yours.

9. Don't tell lies that will hurt another person.

10. Don't be jealous of what others have.

God gave those rules to Moses long ago for the Israelites, but they are still good rules for us today.

Leviticus tells about the

Levites who were priests and about the sacrifices that were offered to God.

The priests were responsible for offering sacrifices to show God that the people were sorry for their sins. They made sure that people worshipped God in the right way and that they kept God's laws.

Numbers tells about counting the Israelite people and about wandering in the wilderness.

The Israelites stayed at Mount Sinai for a year. During this time they took a census and counted all the people. There were

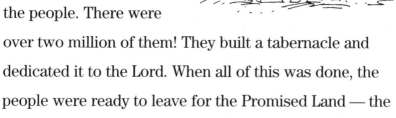

over two million of them! They built a tabernacle and dedicated it to the Lord. When all of this was done, the people were ready to leave for the Promised Land — the special land God had promised them.

God used a cloud and fire to tell the people when to travel. He provided manna for them to eat. But still they grumbled and complained.

Good Times! An Attitude of Gratitude ABC Game

The Israelites spent a lot of time complaining. Sometimes it's easy for us to fall into the grumbling habit. Here's a game you can play with your family and friends to help you develop an attitude of gratitude.

All you need for this is three or more players. The first player thinks of something that starts with an "a" for which she is thankful. For example, "I thank God for apples." The next player adds a "b" word such as "I thank God for apples and brothers." The game continues with each person adding to the list. The game is over when you reach z or when no one can remember the whole list.

Moses Disobeys (Numbers 20)

The people were very thirsty because there was no water to drink. Moses and Aaron prayed to God. God told Moses, "Go and speak to that rock and it will give you water. All of the people and all of the animals will have enough water to drink."

Moses called the people together. He said, "Listen you rebels. We'll bring you water out of this rock." Moses hit the rock twice!

Was this what God told him to do? No! God had told him to speak to the rock, not hit it.

God told Moses, "Since you did not honor me by what you did, you cannot lead the people into the Promised Land."

Moses did not get to enter the Promised Land because he disobeyed God. It might seem a harsh punishment since Moses obeyed God all the other times. But it reminds us that God is very serious about obedience.

Deuteronomy has three sermons that

Moses gave to the people who were going to enter the Promised Land. First, he told them to remember what God had done for them. Second, he told them to understand the laws God had given them.

Third, he told them that obedience is very important. Moses told the people that if they obeyed God they would have rich crops and big herds. They would be healthy and able to defeat their enemies. They would be a great nation as long as they served God.

Moses Dies

Moses was very old by the time the people had wandered in the wilderness all those years. God chose Joshua to be the new leader for the people. Moses was sad that he wouldn't get to enter the Promised Land, but God let Moses see the land from the top of a mountain.

After Moses saw the Promised Land, he died. Joshua took over and the people listened to him and served God. For some people, this time of change was frightening. Unscramble Joshua's message below and write each word on a grape so that you can remember it when you are afraid.

Numbers
14:9

The Lord afraid be with. is us Do not.

Old Testament Heroes

Chapter 3

Tales from **Sarah & Katie**

Katie and Sarah sat with their mom looking at photo albums. "We have a lot of relatives," Katie said. Her teacher had asked the class to find out about their ancestors for a social studies project.

"I don't even know most of them," Sarah said.

"You might not know them," Mom said. "But they still play a big part in who you are."

"Will you tell us about some of them?" Katie asked. "My teacher gave us a whole list of things to find out."

"Okay," Mom said. "It's always good to know your family history."

Books of History

The next twelve books in the Bible are books of history. They tell about things that happened to the Israelites long ago. It's important to know these stories because God wants us to learn from all the men and women in the Bible.

Joshua tells about conquering and settling the Promised Land. God chose Joshua to lead the Israelites into the Promised Land after Moses died. But two things stood in the way. They had to cross the Jordan River, and they had to get through the big walls around the city of Jericho.

A Path through the River (Joshua 3)

Read the following rebus story.

Jordan River **Ark of the Covenant** **Priests**

The spies told Joshua everything that had happened.

"God will give us this land," they said. But first the

people had to find a way to cross the .

Just as he always did, God took care of the people.

Do you remember the , the special box that held the

Ten Commandments? The were carrying the Ark of

the Covenant. Joshua told the to step into the .

As soon as the feet touched the water, God

stopped the from flowing so the Israelites could

walk across on dry land. The stood in the

43

until all the people were across. When the 👥 stepped

out on the other side, the water in the 🌊 started

flowing again.

The Walls that Came Crashing Down (Joshua 6)

The people safely crossed the river. Now it was time to conquer Jericho. God had a plan. He told Joshua to have the people walk around the city once a day for six days. On the seventh day they were to walk around the city seven times. On their final trip around Jericho, the priests blew their horns and the people shouted. The walls came crashing down! The people obeyed God, and He made them conquerors.

Do You Know? Joshua asked the people to make an important decision. Hold this page up to a mirror to read Joshua's message.

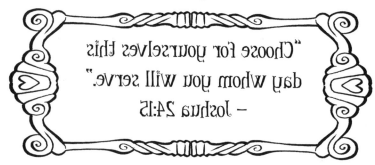

"Choose for yourselves this day whom you will serve."
– Joshua 24:15

Who did Joshua serve?

_____

Who will you serve?

_____

The pictures below show ways that you can serve or worship God. Color the ones you will do this week.

Tales from
Sarah
& Katie

Katie and Sarah sat on their dad's lap talking about their Sunday school lesson. "I don't get it, Dad," Katie said. "After Joshua died it seemed like the people forgot about God unless they were in trouble."

"After God rescued them, they would turn around and do something bad again," Sarah said. "It seems like they should have figured out that it was better to obey God."

"You're right," Dad said. "But they kept going back to their sin. They forgot about God."

"How could they forget about God?" Katie asked. "He parted the Red Sea for them and made the walls of Jericho just fall down!"

"These Israelites were not yet born when those things happened. Their parents should have told them the stories about how God took care of them in the wilderness," Dad said. "That's why Mom and I read Bible stories to you at bedtime each night. You will remember and learn from them."

Judges

tells about the special people God chose as leaders. The people served God while Joshua was alive. They won their battles because they trusted in God. After Joshua died, the people began to worship idols. Everyone did what they wanted rather than what God said was right. This got them in lots of trouble.

The Israelites only called to God when they needed help to defeat their enemies. God picked special people called "judges" to deliver the Israelites.

Gideon (Judges 6-8)

Not all of the judges were brave. In fact, when God asked Gideon to deliver the Israelites from their enemy the Midianites, Gideon was hiding!

God said to Gideon, "Don't be afraid. I will help you beat the Midianites."

Gideon asked, "How can I do that? I'm nobody."

God gave Gideon proof He had chosen him (you can read about that in Judges 6:36-40), so Gideon formed an army. Thousands of men volunteered to be in Gideon's army.

"You don't need that many men," God told Gideon. "Trust me to give you the victory."

✳ Just for Me! ✳

Gideon chose just 300 men to help defeat the Midianites. One night Gideon's army crept quietly to the enemy camp. They had trumpets and pots and torches. When Gideon gave the signal, the men blew their trumpets and smashed their pots. They shouted as loudly as they could and held up their torches. The Midianites thought a large army surrounded them, and they fled. God gave the Israelites the victory.

Draw It! Below is a picture of Gideon's army. Draw a torch in each man's hand.

Why didn't Gideon's army need swords and spears?

_____

_____

If you wrote that God fought the fight for them, you are right.

Samson (Judges 16)

Samson was the strongest man alive. He could tear apart a lion with his bare hands! One time Samson killed a thousand Philistines all by himself. Another time he tore down some city gates that weighed over a thousand pounds. Then he carried them to the top of a hill. Even though Samson had strong muscles, he didn't have a strong will to obey God. Many times he did things that didn't please God.

The Philistines wanted to know the secret of Samson's strength. They paid his friend Delilah to find out. Delilah was a Philistine, an enemy of the Israelites. She was not a good friend for Samson to have. She did not believe in the true God. Samson made up stories about how he got his strength. Finally he told her the truth. God gave him strength as long as he didn't cut his hair. It was a sign of a vow that he would serve God.

Delilah let the Philistines cut Samson's hair while he was asleep and he lost his strength. The Philistines captured and blinded him. They kept him as a prisoner. During his time in prison, Sampson's hair grew again. Samson prayed for his strength to return. God gave him back his strength. Samson pushed over large pillars in a temple of the Philistine's false god. The roof fell down, killing everyone.

These are the stories of only two of the judges. You can read more stories about God's special deliverers in the book of Judges.

Ruth

A woman named Naomi lived in Bethlehem. She and her husband had two sons. One year there was not enough food to eat in Bethlehem. Naomi and her husband and their two sons went to a nearby country named Moab. There was plenty of food to eat in Moab.

Naomi's husband died while they were in this land. Her two sons married Moabite women. Then the two sons died. Naomi and her two daughters-in-law were left to care for themselves.

Naomi decided to return to Bethlehem. "We'll go with you," Ruth and Orpah said.

"No. You need to go and find new husbands," Naomi said.

Orpah left. But Ruth said, "I will go wherever you go. I will serve your God." Ruth was a Moabite. They worshipped idols. Ruth wanted to worship the one true God.

Back then, poor people could go into fields and gather the leftover grain from fields. Ruth went to the field owned by Boaz. He saw Ruth and told his workers to leave extra grain for her to pick up. Ruth and Naomi always had enough to eat.

Boaz loved Ruth, and he married her. They had a son named Obed. He was King David's grandfather.

1 & 2 Samuel

The books of First and Second Samuel continue with Israel's history. They begin with the birth of Samuel, who was the last judge and also the first prophet. They are full of exciting stories about Samuel, King Saul, and David.

Hannah's Baby (I Samuel 1)

Read the rebus story using the story key below.

Baby   **Temple**

Hannah loved God, but she was sad because she wanted a . Once a year Hannah's family went to the to worship. While they were at the , Hannah prayed for a .

Eli, the priest, saw Hannah. He asked her what was wrong. Hannah told him that she wanted a . Eli said, "Go in peace, and may the God of Israel grant you what you have asked of him."

God answered Hannah's prayer and gave her a . She named him Samuel, meaning, "Asked of God." When Samuel was old enough, Hannah took him to the and dedicated him to the Lord's work.

Israel's First King (I Samuel 8-10)

Remember the special deliverers in the book of Judges? Samuel was a good judge who listened to God and helped the people love and serve God. But now Samuel was old and the people wanted a king like all the countries around them. God wanted to be their king, but they rejected God as king.

Samuel anointed Saul as king. Saul was tall and strong and people liked having him as their king. As long as King Saul listened when Samuel told him what God wanted him to do, he was successful.

God Rejects Saul (I Samuel 15)

At first Saul was a good king and listened to God. Then the Israelites attacked the Amalekites. Samuel told King Saul that God had commanded that all the Amalekites and all their belongings be destroyed. Saul disobeyed. He kept some of the best sheep and cattle. He pretended that they were to be a sacrifice to God.

He also spared Agag, the king.

Samuel found out and told King Saul that he would be replaced as king. One of his sons would not get to be king after him. A king would be chosen from another family.

Do you know? What did Samuel tell Saul about obedience? On each line, write the letter that comes between the two letters to read the message.

___ ___   ___ ___ ___ ___   ___ ___

su   np   np   ac   df   xz   hj   rt

___ ___ ___ ___ ___ ___

ac   df   su   su   df   qs

___ ___ ___ ___

su   gi   zb   mo

___ ___ ___ ___ ___ ___ ___ ___ ___ .

rt   zb   bd   qs   hj   eg   hj   bd   df

— 1 Samuel 15:22

This verse means that it is better to do what God wants us to do rather than to disobey and then ask Him for forgiveness.

A New King is Chosen (I Samuel 16)

Since King Saul had disobeyed, someone was chosen from another family to be king. God told Samuel to go to Jesse's house. "I have chosen one of his sons to be king," God told Samuel. "You are to anoint the one I show you." Samuel went to see Jesse. One by one the sons walked past Samuel, but God did not show Samuel which of the sons was to be king.

"The Lord has not chosen these," Samuel said to Jesse. "Are these all the sons you have?"

Jesse told Samuel that he had a younger son who was tending the sheep. Samuel told Jesse to send for his youngest son, David.

When David stood before Samuel, God said, "Rise and anoint him; he is the one."

Samuel anointed David, but it would be a long time before David actually became the king.

On the following page, David the shepherd boy is in the field playing his harp and singing praises to God. However, twelve of his sheep have hidden in the maze. Follow the paths to help David find the twelve sheep.

David Fights Goliath (I Samuel 17)

During the time David was waiting to be king, Saul's army was at war with the Philistines. Every morning and evening, a giant named Goliath shouted a challenge to the Israelites. He said if one of them could defeat him, the Philistines would be their servants. But if Goliath won, the Israelites would serve the Philistines.

David heard this and went to King Saul. David told the king that he had killed both a lion and a bear while tending sheep and that he would fight Goliath.

Saul said, "Go and the Lord be with you." Saul offered David his armor, but David refused. He wasn't used to it. Besides, he knew God would be with him.

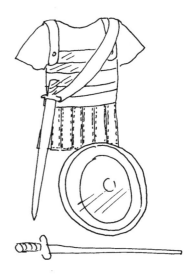

David took his sling and five smooth stones from the stream and approached Goliath.

Goliath looked at David and mocked him. "Am I a dog, that you come at me with sticks?"

David answered, "This day the Lord will hand you over to me."

David slung the first stone at Goliath. It hit him in the forehead, and Goliath fell to the ground. David ran and killed Goliath with his own sword. When the Philistines saw this, they all fled.

Make It!

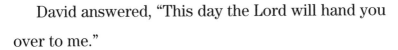

❂ Trust Stone ❂

The Israelite army was afraid of Goliath. We may not face a giant, but there are things that we are all afraid of. Just as God

helped David defeat Goliath, God will help us defeat
the things that make us afraid. This project will help
you remember that God is with you just as he was
with David.

 ## You Need:

✳ One smooth stone just like David used to defeat
   Goliath — make sure that it is big enough to decorate

✳ Paint in your favorite colors

✳ Paint brush

✳ Marker

✳ Newspapers to work on

When I am afraid,
I will trust in you.
Psalm 56:3

 ## To Do:

✳ Wash your stone and let it dry.

✳ Paint the stone your favorite color. Let it dry.

✳ Paint the stone a second time if needed and let dry.

✳ Write these words on the stone: "When I am afraid,
   I will trust in you." — Psalm 56:3

✳ Decorate any way you desire.

✳ Set the stone where it can remind you that God is
   always with you, even when you are afraid or need
   to defeat your own giant.

Saul is Jealous (I Samuel 19-24)

Now David was a hero. He
became an officer in the army, and
all the people loved him. Saul's son
Jonathan was David's best friend.
They were good friends. But Saul
was jealous of David. As David
became more popular, Saul became
more and more angry with him.
Finally Saul tried to kill David.
David had to hide in caves in the
wilderness. David had chances to
kill Saul, but he never did. He knew that would not
honor God. David trusted God to work things out.

David Becomes King (2 Samuel 2-7)

Saul died on the battlefield and David became king.
First he was king over only Judah, the two southern
tribes. One of Saul's sons reigned over the ten northern
tribes. Later David took over those tribes and ruled all
twelve tribes. He made Jerusalem the capital city. David
wanted to build a beautiful temple for God, but God told
David he couldn't build it. One of David's sons would be
the one to build it.

1 & 2 Kings

In these books you can read about good kings and wicked kings, good prophets and false prophets. You'll also read about how God allowed His people to be captured because they disobeyed Him so many times.

Solomon is Wise (I Kings 3)

Solomon became king after David died. Solomon showed his love for God by obeying him and offering sacrifices. God was pleased with Solomon. God appeared to him in a dream telling him, "Ask for whatever you want Me to give you."

You might expect a king to ask for power or fame or money. What did Solomon ask for? To find out, look at the paw print under each line. Write the letter that goes with each paw print.

A=   E=   H=   I=

R=   S=   T=   W=

Solomon asked for wisdom to rule the people well. God said He would give Solomon a wise heart and that He would also give him riches and honor. People came from all over to get Solomon's advice and help with problems.

The Temple (1 Kings 5-9)

Solomon built a very grand temple for God. Thousands of people worked on the temple. The floors and walls were made of stone and cedar wood covered with gold. In front of the temple there was a large porch with two pillars. When the temple was done, the Ark of the Covenant (the special box that held the

Ten Commandments) was placed in it. King Solomon and all the people celebrated for two weeks. God promised to protect Solomon and his people as long as they obeyed Him.

The Kingdom is Divided (1 Kings 11-16)

Solomon started out as a good king who loved and obeyed God. Later, he started worshipping idols. God told Solomon that he would lose most of his kingdom. After Solomon died, much of the kingdom would be taken away from his son. It would be given to one of Solomon's leaders, Jeroboam.

Solomon tried to kill Jeroboam. Jeroboam escaped to Egypt and stayed there until Solomon was dead. Rehoboam, Solomon's son, was made king over the two tribes that made up Judah. Jeroboam was king over the ten tribes that made up Israel. The kingdoms often fought with each other.

Elijah and the Prophets of Baal (1 Kings 17-22)

King Ahab and his wife Jezebel worshipped the god Baal. They made him the official god of the Northern Kingdom, Israel. Elijah went to King Ahab with a message. Elijah told him it wouldn't rain for many years because he was so wicked. Everyone became hungry because food won't grow without rain.

After a long time without rain, it was time for a

showdown between God and Baal. Elijah built an altar to God at the top of Mount Carmel. King Ahab built one for Baal. The 450 prophets of Baal called on Baal to send fire and burn up a bull that was offered on the altar. They cried and called on Baal for hours but nothing happened.

Then Elijah poured twelve large jars of water over his altar with the bull sacrificed on it. Then Elijah prayed to God. Immediately the altar was consumed by fire. Even the wood and the stones and dirt under it burned up!

The people believed in Elijah's God and the prophets of Baal were destroyed.

The Northern Kingdom is Captured
(2 Kings 17)

The kings of Israel, the Northern Kingdom, were sinful. They worshipped false gods. They disobeyed God's laws. Finally God's patience with them ran out and He allowed them to be captured by Assyria. They had to go live in a foreign land while other people lived in their land.

The Southern Kingdom is Captured
(2 Kings 25)

King Joash loved God, but not all the kings that came after him did. Some of them were wicked. One King, Ahaz, even sacrificed his own son to a false god. He stole silver and gold from the temple. Then he closed the temple.

His son, Hezekiah, was a good king. He reopened the temple and encouraged people to worship God. When the Assyrians tried to capture them, an angel defeated them.

Two bad kings reigned after Hezekiah. Then young king Josiah took the throne. He found the Book of the Law, which had been lost, and read it to the people. Things were good while Josiah reigned. But after Josiah, there were more wicked kings. God allowed the Babylonians to conqueror Judah. The people were taken to Babylon to live but God promised that it would only be for 70 years. You'll read more about this later.

1 & 2 Chronicles These books repeat much of

the history of the southern kingdom already told in
1&2 Samuel and 1&2 Kings.

The first chapters of 1 Chronicles give us the list of
David's ancestors. It goes on to tell about David's reign
as king.

Second Chronicles retells stories about the reign of
Solomon. It tells about other rulers of Judah.

The book ends 70 years later when the king of Persia
(the Persians conquered Babylon so now they were in
charge) allowed the people to return to Jerusalem to
rebuild the temple in Jerusalem.

Do You Remember? You've read about many

people so far in the books of history. Do you remember
who did what? Choose the correct name from the word
bank for each question.

WORD BANK: Gideon   Joash   David
Solomon   Joshua   Samuel   Moses

1. This baby was hidden in a basket in the river.

_____

2. This child heard God call his name in the night.

_____

3. He led the people into the Promised Land.

_____

4. He led 300 soldiers against the Midianites.

_____

5. This shepherd boy became a king.

_____

6. He asked God for wisdom.

_____

7. This child was hidden in the temple for six years to save his life.

_____

Ezra Ezra begins where 2 Chronicles ends with God's people being allowed to return to Jerusalem to rebuild the temple.

God's people had to stay in Babylon for many years. When Cyrus became king of Persia, things began to improve. Cyrus told the Jewish captives in Babylon that they could return to Jerusalem to rebuild the temple. He made sure that all the things that had been taken from the temple were returned.

When the people arrived in Jerusalem, they dedicated the new temple site to God. They rebuilt the altar and offered sacrifices to God.

Building materials were gathered and the work of laying the temple's foundation began. After the foundation stones were laid, the people sang and shouted for joy. The work stopped for a while because of enemies, but it was finally completed after many years.

Nehemiah This book is named for Nehemiah, who was cupbearer for the Persian king. The king had to trust his cupbearer because the cupbearer made sure he wasn't poisoned.

Tales from **Sarah & Katie** Katie and Sarah were watching the news with their parents. There was a special report on hurricane damage in Florida. They saw pictures of homes and buildings that had been destroyed.

"It looks like the whole city is ruined," Katie said.

"What are all those people going to do?" Sarah asked. "Where will they live?"

"They will have to rebuild their houses and businesses," Dad said. "Church and community groups will help. Sometimes strangers donate money to help the people rebuild."

"I can't believe that a city can be destroyed like that," Katie said. "The people must be really sad."

"They are," Dad said. "It reminds me of Nehemiah."

"Who is that?" Sarah asked.

"He was a man of God who lived in Old Testament times. Jerusalem had been captured because the people weren't following God. God's people had to leave Jerusalem and other people moved in. When God's people were allowed to return they found it a mess! The temple was ruined and the city walls and gates were destroyed."

"And Nehemiah lived there?" Katie asked.

"He was a cup bearer for a king in Persia. When he heard how bad it was in Jerusalem, he asked to go help clean it up and rebuild. He was very sad when he saw Jerusalem in ruins. He organized the people to rebuild the walls."

Esther

Esther is the well-known story of a brave queen who saved her people.

King Xerxes of Persia was having a celebration. He wanted Queen Vashti to take part in the celebration. But the queen wouldn't come. The king was used to getting his own way, so Queen Vashti was sent away from the palace.

The king chose Esther to be his new queen. Esther was young, kind, and beautiful. She was also a Jew. Mordecai, a relative of Esther's, also worked in the palace. He told her not to tell anyone that she was a Jew.

The king's chief minister, Haman, hated the Jews. He told the king that the Jews were troublemakers who broke the law. He talked the king into a plan to kill the Jews.

Mordecai told Esther about the evil plan. Mordecai said to her, "Perhaps you are there for such a time as this." He thought God had put Esther there to save her people.

Esther invited the king to a banquet and asked him to

bring Haman. At the first banquet, she asked them to attend another banquet the next night.

Haman was happy after the first banquet. Haman thought he was very important and that people should bow down to him. Mordecai wouldn't bow to him. Haman was angry! He decided to have Mordecai killed and built gallows to have Mordecai hanged.

At the second banquet, Esther told the king about Haman's plan against the Jews. Haman was hanged on the gallows that he built for Modecai. The Jews were allowed to defend themselves against their enemies. They celebrated with feasting and joy.

Mordecai told Esther that she might have been at the palace "for such a time as this." God put her there so that she could be there at just the right time to help her people. Do you remember another person God put somewhere at just the right time to help others? Joseph. His brothers were cruel and sold him but God used Joseph to warn the leaders about a famine and to save enough food to survive. He was able to help his own family to have enough food.

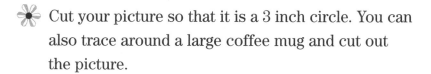

❂ For Such a Time as This ❂

Make It!

God can use you right where you are "for such a time as this" also. This photo frame can help you remember that.

 You Need:

❋ Old CD — ask for permission first

❋ Glue

❋ Photo of yourself

❋ Scissors

❋ Magnet or strip of magnetic tape

❋ Marker

❋ Stickers or markers to decorate the CD

 To Do:

❋ Cut your picture so that it is a 3 inch circle. You can also trace around a large coffee mug and cut out the picture.

❋ Glue the picture to the shiny side of the CD.

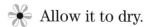
✸ Allow it to dry.

✸ Write the words "For such a time as this" around the bottom of the CD below your picture.

✸ Add any decorations you desire.

✸ Glue the magnet to the back, or attach magnet tape.

✸ Allow it to dry.

✸ Hang your picture on the refrigerator or another place where it will remind you that God can use you right where you are.

Songs and Sayings

Chapter 4

Tales from
Sarah
& Katie*

Sarah entered the house and slammed the door behind her.

"What's wrong?" her mother asked. "Usually you come home from school happy."

"Not today. I lost my math homework. I told the teacher I'd done it, but she said since I didn't have it, she couldn't count it. Then I missed two really easy words on the spelling test. At lunch I knocked my carton of

milk over, and it got on my pants. I had to wear wet pants all afternoon. It's been a horrible day!" Sarah said. "Nobody could have a worse day than I did!"

"I feel bad that you had such a hard day. But someone once had a worse day than you. His name was Job. He was a good man but a lot of bad stuff happened to him. His children and animals died. And he got sores on his skin," Mom said.

"It sounds like he had some really bad days," Sarah said.

"He did. But God blessed him in the end," Mom said.

Books of Poetry

The five books of the Bible starting with the book of Job are called the Books of Poetry.

Job (say it with a long "o"— like "Jobe") is about a good man who had a lot of bad things happen to him.

Bad Things Happen to Job

Job was a rich farmer who loved God. Even though Job appears later in the Bible, Job lived at about the same time as Abraham in Genesis. Job lived a happy and good life. God was pleased with Job because Job obeyed God and was kind to other people. One day Satan said to God, "Job only obeys You because You give him good things."

God let Satan test Job by taking away his family and possessions. All of his animals were either stolen or killed. His children died. Job still loved God and served Him. Even after his body was covered with sores, Job still trusted God.

Because of Job's faith, God blessed him with more animals and children than he had before.

Tales from Sarah & Katie

"Do you have a favorite poem?" Katie asked her mom.

"I can't think of one right now," she said. "Why are you asking?"

"We have to memorize a poem for school," Katie said. "The teacher said it can be any poem we want."

"I can't think of a poem like that," Mom said. "But I do have a favorite passage from the books of poetry in the Bible. It's Psalm 23, the Shepherd's Psalm."

"I like Psalm 23, too. Maybe I will ask my teacher if I can memorize that instead of a rhyming poem," Katie said.

Psalms are praises to God. Some are happy, some are sad. Some ask God for help, some praise him for his goodness. David wrote many of the Psalms.

Here are some of the words David wrote to praise God:

"O Lord, our Lord, how majestic is your name in all the earth!" — Psalm 8:1

"I will praise you, O Lord, with all my heart; I will tell of all your wonders. I will be glad and rejoice in you; I will sing praise to your name, O Most High." — Psalm 9:1-2

"I love you, O Lord, my strength. Therefore I will praise you among the nations, O Lord; I will sing praises to your name." — Psalm 18:1, 49

Try this

Sarah wrote her own psalm:

You are with me when I am having a good day and when I am having a bad day.

You give me joy in my heart on rainy days and a song in my heart on sunny days.

You always take care of me and are always with me. I love you God.

Write your own psalm of praise to God on the following lines.

_____

_____

_____

_____

Proverbs
Wise King Solomon wrote the book of Proverbs to share his wisdom. The book of Proverbs has many short, wise sayings to read and follow. Here are some proverbs about families:

"Listen ... to your father's instruction and do not forsake your mother's teaching." — Proverbs 1:8

"A wise son brings joy to his father, but a foolish son grief to his mother." — Proverbs 10:1

"He who spares the rod hates his son, but he who loves him is careful to discipline him." — Proverbs 13:24

Do You Know?
What does Proverbs 15:1 say? Use the code below to discover for yourself.

	1	2	3	4
*	A	E	G	H
^	L	N	R	S
#	T	U	W	Y

___ ___ ___ ___ ___ ___ ___   ___ ___ ___ ___ ___ ___

*1   *3 *2 ^2 #1 ^1 *2   *1 ^2 ^4 #3 *2 ^3

___ ___ ___ ___ ___   ___ ___ ___ ___   ___ ___ ___ ___ ___.

#1 #2 ^3 ^2 ^4   *1 #3 *1 #4   #3 ^3 *1 #1 *4

What do you think that means?

_____

_____

_____

The next time you are having an argument, try giving a kind and gentle answer and see what happens.

Ecclesiastes Solomon wrote this book to talk about life's meaning.

Solomon started out as a good king who worshipped God. Later Solomon married many foreign wives. He started worshipping their false gods. Solomon learned that life without God is empty.

Solomon wrote, *"Fear God and keep his commandments, for this is the whole duty of man"* (Ecclesiastes 12:13). He was telling us that obeying God is the most important thing that we can do.

How do you obey God each day?

_____

_____

_____

_____

Song of Songs

Solomon wrote this book as a love song to his true love. It is sometimes called the "Song of Solomon."

Many people believe that Solomon wrote Song of Songs to his one true love before he began to marry other wives. Marrying several wives was common back

then. Solomon writes about how beautiful it is to be married to someone you love.

Even though these books of the Bible are different from the books of history or law, we can learn from them. The Psalms are especially popular because they are easy to read and understand. People get comfort in difficult times from the psalms. They also remind us to praise God.

The last books in the Old Testament are the books of prophecy. These were God's warnings to people about things to come if they didn't change their ways. The stories of Daniel, the Fiery Furnace, and Jonah are all in the books of prophecy so keep reading!

God's Messengers – Part One

Chapter 5

Tales from Sarah & Katie

Katie and Sarah watched as their dad and older brother, Jesse, built a tree house for them. It was going to be their special place to play, read books, and do homework.

"Be careful or you'll fall," Dad called to Jesse. Jesse was in the tree nailing down boards for the floor. Dad

was on the ground getting more supplies.

"I'm okay," Jesse answered. "I have good balance."

"I really think you need to hold on," Dad said.

Jesse finished nailing the nail and reached for another one. As he stretched to get it, his foot slipped off the branches. Jesse felt himself falling. He tried to grab hold of a branch but missed. Jesse landed on the ground with a thud!

Katie and Sarah ran over to him.

"Are you okay?" Dad asked.

"I think so. I would feel better if I had listened to you

and held on, though," Jesse admitted.

"That's kind of like the Israelites that we've been learning about," Dad said. "God warned them over and over to obey his commands. He even sent special people called prophets to give them warnings."

"But they didn't listen, just like me," Jesse said.

"Yes, only worse things happened to them than falling out of a tree," Dad said.

The Major Prophets

The rest of the books of the Old Testament are the Major and Minor Prophets. They're not called Major and Minor because some are more important than others. The Major Prophets are just longer books than the Minor Prophets.

Isaiah Isaiah was a prophet to the two tribes that made up the Southern Kingdom, Judah.

Sometimes Judah had a king who served God. Other times they had a king who worshipped idols. In the first half of his book, Isaiah warned the people that they would be captured if they didn't change their ways.

The second half of the book is full of hope and reminds us of God's promises and faithfulness. The book of Isaiah told of a coming Savior who would save the world from their sins.

Who is that Savior?

_____

That's right! Jesus is the Savior of the world. Add Baby Jesus to the picture below.

Jeremiah

Jeremiah was also a prophet to the Southern Kingdom.

One of the kings of Judah wanted to please God. His name was Josiah. He became king when he was only eight years old! God sent Jeremiah to help Josiah. But the kings that came after Josiah didn't love God. Jeremiah told them that God would punish them for serving idols.

He said that Babylon would take them captive. The people got so angry with Jeremiah that they threw him in prison!

Jeremiah was called "The Weeping Prophet" because he was sad about the punishment that God would give the people.

God's Promise

Even while God's people were being punished for their disobedience, God hadn't forgotten about them. He gave them a special promise. Look at the letter under each line. In each space, write the letter that comes after that letter in the alphabet. What does the message say?

____ ____ ____ ____ ____ ____ ____ ____
  E   N   Q   H   J   M   N   V

____ ____ ____ ____ ____ ____ ____ ____
  S   G   D   O   K   Z   M   R

____ ____ ____ ____ ____ ____ ____ ____
  H   G   Z   U   D   E   N   Q

____ ____ ____ ... ____ ____ ____ ____ ____
  X   N   T   O   K   Z   M   R

____ ____ ____ ____ ____ ____ ____ ____ ____
  S   N   F   H   U   D   X   N   T

____ ____ ____ ____ ____ ____ ____
  G   N   O   D   Z   M   C

____ ____ ____ ____ ____ ____ ____.
  Z   E   T   S   T   Q   D

— Jeremiah 29:11

Just as God had a good plan for the Jews, he has a wonderful plan for you too.

Lamentations This is a sad book written by Jeremiah about the destruction of Jerusalem.

Jeremiah was unhappy because Jerusalem was destroyed. Even the beautiful temple was gone. There were fires burning everywhere, and people were lying dead in the streets. Jeremiah wrote about these sad things in the book of Lamentations.

Ezekiel Ezekiel was a prophet to the Jews while they were captives in Babylon.

Ezekiel was in the first group of captives taken to Babylon. Ezekiel is best known for the visions God used to show him about the future. One of the visions was about dry bones (Ezekiel 37:1-8). Another vision was about wheels within wheels (Ezekiel 1:15-21). Ezekiel was very dramatic and liked to act out messages from God.

Daniel

Daniel and his three friends were among a special group of captives sent from Judah to Babylon. They were trained to serve in the king's palace.

One night the king had a dream, and he didn't know what it meant. He wanted someone to explain it to him, but he wouldn't tell anyone what the dream was. He said they must tell him both the dream and its meaning.

God showed Daniel the dream. It was of a statue with a head of gold, chest and arms of silver, belly and thighs of bronze, legs of iron, and feet of iron and clay.

Daniel explained to the king that he was the head of gold but after him other weaker kingdoms would come. Finally God would set up his own kingdom and destroy all other kingdoms.

The Fiery Furnace (Daniel 3)

The king remembered the big statue in his dream. He thought it would be a good idea to make a statue of himself out of gold. It was ninety feet tall!

"Everyone must bow down to my statue when the music plays," the king said.

"Anyone who doesn't bow down will be thrown into a blazing hot furnace."

What would you do if you were there when the music played?

_____

_____

_____

_____

Daniel was away when the king made this decree, but his friends Shadrach, Meshach, and Abednego were there. When the music played, they were the only ones not to bow down.

"We will not worship a statue," they said. "We only worship the true God."

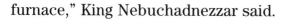

"You will be thrown into the furnace," King Nebuchadnezzar said.

"The God we serve is able to rescue us from it," the three said.

The king was angry. He ordered the furnace heated seven times hotter than usual. It was so hot it killed the soldiers who threw them into it.

"Didn't we throw three men into the furnace?" the king exclaimed. "There are four men walking around in the furnace."

The king ordered the three friends to come out of the furnace. "Your God has saved you," he said. "He is the God we will worship."

The Lion's Den
(Daniel 6)

When Daniel was about 80 years old, he was thrown into a lion's den for praying. But he was not harmed!

Why did the lions not eat Daniel?

_____

_____

That's right! The angels shut the lions' mouths. Daniel said, *"My God sent his angel, and he shut the mouths of the lions. They have not hurt me, because I was found innocent in his sight. Nor have I ever done any wrong before you, O king."* — Daniel 6:21

God's Messengers – Part Two

Chapter 6

Tales from
Sarah & Katie

Katie and Sarah sat on the bleachers next to their mom and dad and brother Jesse. Their older sister, Jenni, was on the girl's basketball team. This was the championship game. Katie and Sarah waited excitedly for the teams to come out from the locker rooms. Suddenly everyone stood up cheering as the girls' basketball teams ran onto the court.

"Wow, the players really look ready for this game," Sarah said.

"Yes, they do," Dad agreed. "They're going to announce the starting line up now."

The prophets are God's starting line up to give others his messages. You read about the five major prophets already. There were also twelve Minor Prophets on God's team.

The Minor Prophets

Hosea God called Hosea to go to Israel, the Northern Kingdom. Hosea tells of God's love for Israel even though they worshipped false gods. It's also a picture of how Jesus came to die for our sins and make us His own.

☼ Jesus Saves Us Pencil Topper ☼

This pencil topper is not just colorful and fun, it also tells the story of Jesus' love for us.

 **You Need:**

 New pencil with eraser

❋ Ribbon about ⅛" wide — about 8 inches for each tassel you want on your pencil

❋ Pony beads (small plastic beads with a hole for stringing) — black, red, white, yellow and green — one per tassel

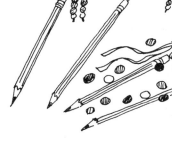

❋ Glue

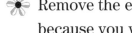 **To Do:**

❋ Remove the eraser from the pencil. Be careful because you will use the eraser later.

 Take the black bead and put the ribbon through it. Center the black bead in the middle of the ribbon.

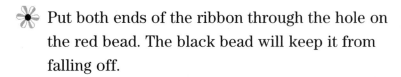

✳ Put both ends of the ribbon through the hole on the red bead. The black bead will keep it from falling off.

✳ Put the white bead on, then the yellow, and finally the green.

✳ Put a dab of glue on the ends of the ribbon. Put the gluey ends of ribbon in the eraser hole.

✳ Carefully put the eraser back on the pencil.

✳ You can make as many tassels for your pencil as you like.

✳ When people ask about your pencil tassel, you can tell them:

Black is for the sin in our hearts.

Red is for the blood Jesus shed on the cross for us.

White is the color of our heart when we ask Jesus to forgive our sin.

Yellow reminds us of the streets of gold in heaven where we will be with Jesus some day.

Green reminds us that we grow in our faith by reading our Bible, praying and going to church.

Joel

God called Joel to go to Judah, the Southern Kingdom. There was a huge swarm of locusts that ate all the green plants in Judah so there was no food to eat. At the same time, there was no rain! Joel told the people that this was God's judgment because of their sins.

Joel encouraged the people to confess their sins and turn back to God before it was too late.

Amos

Amos gave his prophecy to Israel, the Northern Kingdom.

Amos listed for the people the things that they were doing wrong. He told them that they would be punished but that after they were taken captive, they would return to their own land.

Obadiah

God sent Obadiah to Edom, an enemy of Judah.

The people of Edom hated the people of Judah. When Babylon captured Judah, the Edomites helped the Babylonians. They stole things from Judah. Obadiah told the people of Edom that God would punish them. He told them that they would lose their land to their enemies.

Jonah

God sent Jonah to Nineveh, the capital of Assyria, to talk to the people there because they were leading sinful lives. God wanted Jonah to tell them to stop doing wrong. Jonah didn't want to so he tried to hide from God.

However, God arranged for Jonah to spend three days in the belly of a big fish. After that, Jonah decided that it would be much better to obey God!

Micah

God called Micah to take his message to Judah, the Southern Kingdom.

Micah told the people what God required of them. He said, *"And what does the Lord require of you? To act justly and to love mercy and to walk humbly with your God."* — Micah 6:8

Which of These Things can you do

this week to walk with God? Put an x beside the things
you will do.

_____ Read my Bible

_____ Pray

_____ Participate during family devotions

_____ Ask my parents or Sunday school teacher
questions to help me understand the Bible better

_____ Tell my friends about Jesus

_____ Ask a friend to go to church with me

Nahum Nahum went to Nineveh about 150 years
after Jonah had gone there.

When Jonah had talked to the people of Nineveh 150
years earlier, they turned from their sinful ways and
worshipped God. This time the people of Nineveh ignored
God's message. They were wicked and cruel. Nahum
warned them that they would be punished.

Habakkuk Habakkuk gave his message to Judah,
the Southern Kingdom.

The book of Habakkuk is a book of questions and
answers. Habakkuk asked God questions and God answered
him. The questions and answers were something like this:

Q: Why aren't the people of Judah being punished for the sinful way they are living?

A: They will be punished by the Babylonians.

Q: The Babylonians are worse than the people of Judah. How can you use them to punish Judah?

A: Babylon will be punished later.

God's answers helped Habakkuk understand what God planned. Then Habakkuk praised God for his power.

Do You Know? What did Habakkuk say after he understood God's plan?

Use this key to find the answer:

1=A	2=B	3=D	4=E
5=F	6=G	7=I	8=J
9=L	10=M	11=N	12=O
13=R	14=S	15=T	16=U
17=V	18=W	19=Y	

___ ___ ___ ___ ___ ___ ___
7   18   7   9   9   2   4

___ ___ ___ ___ ___ ___ ___ ___
8   12   19   5   16   9   7   11

___ ___ ___ ___ ___
6   12   3   10   19

___ ___ ___ ___ ___ ___. — Habakkuk 3:18
14   1   17   7   12   13

Zephaniah

Zephaniah was the last prophet to Judah before the Babylonians captured them.

Zephaniah's message to Judah was both one of sorrow and one of singing. First Zephaniah tells the people that God would punish them by allowing them to be taken captive. But the book of Zephaniah ends with the promise that the people would return to their own land, and that God would bless them.

Haggai

God sent Haggai to the Jews after they returned from their 70 years of captivity in Babylon.

The Jews who returned to Jerusalem were supposed to rebuild the temple. They laid the foundation but they didn't finish the actual temple. Their land had been destroyed and their fields were filled with weeds. The people had to clear the fields and rebuild their homes. They didn't bother to work on the temple.

God sent Haggai to tell them to get working on the temple again. Haggai encouraged them as they worked.

Zechariah

Zechariah was also sent to the Jews in Jerusalem after the captivity. He was there at the same time as Haggai.

God spoke to Zechariah in many visions. The visions told of both the restoring of Jerusalem and of the coming of Jesus in the future. Zechariah said that Jesus would be the Savior of the world and then the judge of the world.

Malachi

Malachi was probably the last prophet to speak to the people of Israel and Judah after the captivity.

When the people returned from being captives, they again started to worship idols. Malachi told the people to turn back to God, and he told them of a coming Savior. The Savior that Malachi said would come is Jesus.

Four hundred years

Jesus was born 400 years after Malachi gave the people his message of a coming Savior. During these 400 years no one spoke or wrote messages from God. After the 400 years of no messages from God, the New Testament starts with the birth of the promised Savior.

All About Jesus

Chapter 7

Tales from
Sarah
&Katie

"Are you ready?" Dad asked Katie and Sarah.

"Yes," they answered excitedly.

"Okay, turn out the lights," Dad said. When it was dark, he plugged in the extension cord, and Christmas lights lit up the room.

"Wow," Katie and Sarah said.

"Beautiful," Mom agreed.

"The lights remind us that Jesus came to be the light of the world," Dad said. Then he opened his Bible and read the Christmas story aloud.

The gospels tell us about Jesus' life. Two of them begin with his birth. The others start when He is older.

The Gospels

The first four books of the New Testament are called "The Gospels." They tell about Jesus' life, death, and resurrection.

Because the four gospels tell many of the same stories about Jesus, we aren't going to look at each book separately. Instead we are going to go through Jesus' life and look at some of the most important events. We won't be able to talk about every story in the gospels because that would take up a whole book by itself. But you can read them for yourself in your Bible.

Jesus' Birth (Matthew 1, Luke 1–2)

Mary was a young woman who lived in a small town called Nazareth. She was engaged to be married to a carpenter named Joseph. One day the angel Gabriel appeared to Mary. He said, "God is pleased with you. You will have a child and will call his name Jesus."

"How can this happen?" Mary asked.

"God's Spirit will make it happen," the angel told her.

The angel also went to Joseph and told him to go ahead and marry Mary because her baby would be a special child.

Mary went to visit her cousin Elizabeth. Elizabeth and her husband Zechariah were also expecting a baby. Mary and Elizabeth rejoiced together about this.

Do You Know? What had Zechariah been told to name the baby? Color the spaces with a dot inside to find out.

Near the time that Mary was to have her baby, Augustus, the Roman emperor, decided that everybody should go to their hometown to be counted. Mary and Joseph had to travel to Bethlehem.

It was a long and hot journey to Bethlehem. Night was coming, and Mary and Joseph needed to find a place to stay. Every inn was full of travelers! A kind innkeeper said he had no room to give them, but that they could sleep in the stable. That night Mary gave birth to her baby and named Him Jesus as she had been told. She wrapped Him in swaddling clothes and placed Him in a manger.

Some shepherds were out guarding their sheep that night. Suddenly the dark night was full of bright light! An angel appeared. "I have good news," the angel said. "Tonight a Savior has been born. He is Christ the Lord. Go to Bethlehem, and you will find Him in a stable."

Suddenly a whole group of angels appeared. They said, *"Glory to God in the highest, and on earth peace to men on whom his favor rests."* — Luke 2:14

The shepherds did as the angel said. They hurried to Bethlehem and found Mary and Joseph and Baby Jesus in the stable. The shepherds knelt down and worshipped Jesus.

The Wise Men Visit Jesus (Matthew 2)

Wise Men   **King**   **Star**

Some from the east saw a new in the sky. It meant that a special had been born.

The began a journey to find the new .

In Jerusalem, they met King Herod. He pretended to

want to find the new 👳 too. He said, "When you

find Him, come and tell me so I can worship Him,

also." But King Herod didn't want to worship Jesus.

He really wanted to kill the baby 👳. He didn't want

another 👳 to take his place. But King Herod didn't

know that Jesus would be a special kind of 👳 .

The 👳👳👳 left Jerusalem and followed the 🌟 to

Bethlehem. The special star showed the 👳👳👳

where to find Jesus. The 👳👳👳 bowed down and

offered gifts to Him.

God spoke to the 👳👳👳 in a dream. He told them

not to go back to King Herod but to go home another way.

God also warned Mary and Joseph to take Jesus and flee to

Egypt. That was because King Herod planned to kill all of

the baby boys who were the right age to be the new 👳 .

❂ Christmas Story Ornaments ❂

Make It!

The Christmas story is a favorite story for most people. Matthew 1:18-25 and Luke 2:1-20 tell about Jesus' birth. This is an easy project you can do to remember the birth of the Savior.

You Need:

- Plain Christmas ornaments in any color
- Paint pen or craft or fabric paint with a writing tip

To Do:

A Savior has been Born. Luke 2:11

- Find your favorite verse about Jesus' birth from Matthew or Luke.

- Carefully write the verse on a Christmas ornament.

- Decorate the ornament with a picture that goes with the verse.

- If you want, try to do the whole Christmas story on ornaments.

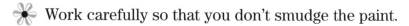

❋ Work carefully so that you don't smudge the paint.

❋ Allow the paint to dry.

❋ Hang on your Christmas tree at Christmas or in another special spot.

Jesus' Childhood (Luke 2)

When Jesus was twelve He traveled with Joseph and Mary to the temple in Jerusalem. When it was time to go home, a whole group started out together. Joseph and Mary thought that Jesus was in the group. After they had traveled a whole day, they discovered that Jesus wasn't with them. They hurried back to Jerusalem and searched for Jesus. Finally they found Him in the temple talking with the teachers. They were amazed at how much Jesus knew.

Jesus' Baptism and Temptation
(Matthew 3-4, Luke 3-4, Mark 1)

Elizabeth's baby, John, was now an adult. He preached to people telling them to be sorry for their sins and turn from them. He told them that a Savior was coming. He baptized the people who turned to God. That's why he is usually called "John the Baptist."

One day Jesus went to the river and asked John to baptize Him.

"You should baptize me," his cousin John said. But he agreed to baptize Jesus.

When Jesus came up out of the water, the heavens opened, and the spirit of God descended like a dove and said, *"This is my Son, whom I love; with Him I am well pleased"* (Matthew 3-17).

After His baptism, Jesus went into the desert for forty days and nights. He didn't have anything to eat during that time. Satan came and tried to tempt Him. Jesus told Satan, "Away from me, Satan! For it is written, 'Worship the Lord your God, and serve him only.'" Satan then left, and angels took care of Jesus.

Fishers of Men (Luke 5)

After Jesus' baptism and temptation, He didn't go back to being a carpenter like before. He started His work telling others about God. One day Jesus went to Galilee where a crowd had gathered to hear Him teach. Jesus sat in a fishing boat and taught the people from the boat.

When He was done speaking to the crowd, Jesus said to Simon Peter, "Let's go out in the deep water and go fishing." James and John were also with them.

Simon Peter said, "We've fished hard all night, and we haven't caught anything. But if You want us to, we'll do it."

Simon Peter, James, and John let down the big net. They caught so many fish in their net that it began to break. The boat was so full of fish that it began to sink!

Jesus said to them, "From now on you will be fishers of men." He meant that Peter, James, and John would help him bring people to God.

Even though the fishermen in Jesus' day were men, everyone can be a fisher of men, including you. Jesus wants us to tell others about Him.

 Make It!

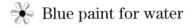 ✿ **Fisherman Bucket** ✿

Here is a fun craft to remind you to be a fisher of men.

▶ You Need:

❋ Small metal bucket (you can also use an empty yogurt container)

❋ Blue paint for water

❋ Green paint

* Fish decals or stickers, or paint to paint fish on the bucket

* Candy worms (optional)

* Clear finish to seal the paint and add shine (optional)

To Do:

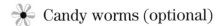

* Paint the outside of bucket or container blue.

* Allow it to dry thoroughly.

* Use the green paint to draw sea grass.

* Allow it to dry thoroughly.

* Add fish stickers or paint fish in the water.

* Allow it to dry.

* Add a coat of clear finish.

* Allow it to dry.

* Fill with candy worms.

* Set it where you can see it to remind you to be a "fisher of men."

Jesus' Special Friends (Mark 3:13-19)

Peter, James, and **John** were three of Jesus' special friends, called disciples. Disciples were followers who helped Him tell others about God. **Peter, James,** and **John** were fishermen. There were nine more disciples. **Andrew** was the brother of Peter. He was also a fisherman. **Matthew** was a tax collector before Jesus called him to be a disciple. Tax collectors weren't always honest but Matthew changed after he met Jesus. **Simon** was a zealot, a person who wanted to turn others against the Romans. **Philip** was another fisherman. **Thomas** is sometimes called

Doubting Thomas because he wanted proof Jesus was risen from the dead. We don't know much about **Thaddeus**, also called **Judas,** or about **Bartholomew** who is also called **Nathanael**, or about another **James** who was not the brother of John. **Judas Iscariot** was the treasurer for the group. He later betrayed Jesus.

Jesus' Miracles

Jesus did many things that He couldn't have done if He weren't the Son of God. Jesus turned water into wine. He raised people from the dead. He healed the lame, deaf, blind, and sick. Jesus calmed a storm and made a small amount of food feed thousands of people. These are just a few of Jesus' miracles.

The Man Through the Roof
(Matthew 9, Mark 2, Luke 5)

One day, some friends wanted to take their friend to Jesus. They carried him on a mat. He couldn't walk, and they believed that Jesus could heal him. Finally they got to the house where Jesus was teaching. There was such a big crowd that the friends couldn't get the sick man anywhere near Jesus!

The friends thought of another plan. They would climb up to the roof of the house. Then they would make a hole and lower their friend into the house. 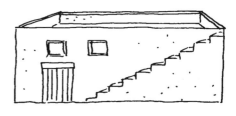 In those days roofs were flat. Sometimes there were even outside stairs up to the rooftop.

113

The friends very carefully cut a hole in the roof. Then they lowered the mat down so it was right in front of Jesus. Jesus saw that the friends believed He could heal the man. Jesus said to the man, "Friend, your sins are forgiven. Take up your mat and go home."

The man stood to his feet. He could walk. He praised Jesus for healing him.

Other Miracles

There are many stories about Jesus' miracles in the gospels. Here are some that you might want to read for yourself. Try reading them from the different gospels.

Jesus Feeds 5,000   Matthew 14:15-21,
                            Mark 6:35-44, Luke 9:12-17,
                            John 6:5-15

Jesus Walks on the Water   Matthew 14:22-33,
                            Mark 6:45-52, John 6:16-21

Jesus Heals the Lepers   Luke 17:11-19

Jesus Raises Lazarus from the dead   John 11:38-45

Jesus' Parables

Sometimes people didn't understand what Jesus was trying to teach them. So He used special stories, called parables, to help them understand.

The Son Who Left Home (Luke 15: 11-32)

This is one of the special stories that Jesus told:

Once there was a rich man with two sons. One day the younger son asked for his share of the money. The father gave him a large amount of money, and the son left home. He spent all his money doing fun and exciting things. But then the money was gone. He had no money and no food, and he was very hungry. The son had to take a job looking after pigs!

The son thought to himself, "Even my father's servants have good food to eat, maybe my father will let me be a servant."

When his father saw him coming, he was so happy that he ran out to meet his son.

The son said, "Father, I have sinned and am no longer worthy to be called your son."

The father forgave his son. He gave him new clothes and planned a feast to celebrate.

The other son was angry. "I have been here the whole

time doing what I should do, but you never had a feast for me!"

"Everything I have is yours," the father said. "Celebrate with us because your brother is home safely."

"God is like that Father. He rejoices when sinners come to Him," Jesus told them.

Make It!

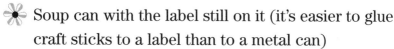

❂ Gift for Dad ❂

Here is a gift you can make to show your dad that you love him. If you don't have a dad, that's okay. You can make this for a teacher, uncle, friend, or even yourself.

You Need:

- ❋ Soup can with the label still on it (it's easier to glue craft sticks to a label than to a metal can)

- ❋ 15 craft sticks

- ❋ Paint in your favorite color

- ❋ Paint brush

- ❋ Glue

- ❋ Two rubber bands

❋ Small piece of craft foam or colored paper

❋ Marker

❋ Stickers or pictures for decoration

❋ Clear finish to seal paint and add shine (optional)

▶ To Do:

❋ Put a thin strip of glue on a craft stick. Press it against the can and move it up and down to spread the glue.

❋ Continue until you have sticks all the way around the can. Make sure the sticks touch each other. If you have trouble keeping them on, put two rubber bands around them and let them dry.

❋ Allow the glue to dry thoroughly.

❋ Paint the sticks in your dad's favorite color (or a color of your choice.)

❋ Allow the paint to dry.

❋ Paint a thin coat of sealer over the paint once it's dry (optional.)

❋ Cut a small triangle out of foam or paper. Write "#1 Dad" or another message on it.

✽ Glue it to the can.

✽ Add stickers, pictures, or other decorations.

✽ Allow it to dry.

✽ Give it to your dad and be sure to tell him how much he means to you. He can use it for pens and pencils or other small items.

Other Stories Jesus Told

There are many more parables that Jesus told. Here are some that you might want to read.

The Good Samaritan	Luke 10:25-37
The Lost Sheep	Matthew 18:10-14
The Talents	Matthew 25:14-30
The Lost Coin	Luke 15:8-10

Jesus' Death

Jesus told people about God and that He was the Son of God. He told them how to live right. Jesus healed people and did other miracles. But not everyone liked Jesus. In fact, some people hated Him. They didn't like to hear that the things they were doing were wrong. They didn't want to turn from their sins. It made them mad when Jesus said He was the Son of God.

At the Jewish feast of the Passover, Jesus shared a special meal with His disciples. This was the last supper they would eat together before His death. Jesus took some bread and told them it was like His body which would be punished for them. He took wine and told them it was like His blood that would be shed for them.

After their last supper together, Jesus went to a garden to pray. While He was praying, Judas led Jesus' enemies to Him. They took Him to the Roman governor, Pontius Pilate. Pilate didn't think that Jesus had done anything wrong, but Jesus' enemies wanted Him to die.

Jesus was nailed to a cross. There were two other men on crosses, one on each side of Jesus. One of the men made fun of Jesus, but the other one believed that Jesus was the Son of God. He asked Jesus to remember him when he went to heaven.

Time passed, and it grew dark even though it was still daytime. Jesus cried out to God, and then He died. Jesus' friends were very sad.

A rich man named Joseph took Jesus' body to a tomb cut in the rock on a hillside. He wrapped Jesus' body in linen cloths and laid Him in the tomb. A huge rock was rolled across the entrance of the tomb. It was a sad day for Jesus' disciples and His friends.

Jesus Comes Back to Life (John 20)

Early Sunday morning one of Jesus' friends named Mary Magdalene went to the tomb. When she got there, Mary saw that the stone was rolled away. The tomb was empty!

Mary ran to find Jesus' followers. "Someone has taken Jesus' body away," she told them. Peter and John

ran to the tomb. They looked inside, but all they saw were the linen cloths that Jesus' body had been wrapped in.

The disciples went back home, but Mary stood by the tomb crying. When Mary looked back in the tomb she saw two angels sitting there. "Why are you crying?" they asked.

"They have taken my Lord away," Mary said.

Mary saw a man standing there. She thought He was the gardener. "Where have you taken Him?" she asked.

The man said, "Mary."

Mary realized that He was not a gardener. It was Jesus standing there! All of Jesus' followers were happy that He was alive again. They were ready to start telling others about Jesus' life, death, and resurrection even if it meant that they would be put in prison!

Exciting Times

Chapter 8

Tales from

Sarah
& Katie

Katie and Sarah stood up to sing the closing song at church.

"Sometimes church seems way too long," Katie said.

"Good thing you didn't live when the church first started," Dad said. "Sometimes the apostles and early Christians would preach for hours."

"Hours? I'd fall asleep," Sarah said.

"Well, a man named Eutychus did just that," Dad said. "Paul was preaching in a house. Eutychus was sitting in a third story window. He fell out of the window."

"Then what?" Sarah asked.

"You'll have to find out for yourself in the book of Acts," Dad said.

Acts

There is only one book of history in the New Testament. It is called Acts. The book of Acts is an exciting book that tells what happened right after Jesus rose from the dead. There are stories about miracles, new believers, missionary journeys, and more!

The Holy Spirit (Acts 1-2)

Jesus went back to heaven forty days after He rose from the dead. He told His followers to wait for the Holy Spirit to come and give them power and strength to start the early church.

On the Day of Pentecost, Jesus' disciples were all together. Judas was no longer with them. Matthias took his place. Suddenly a sound like a rushing wind filled the room.

A flame of fire came down on each follower's head, and they were filled with God's Spirit. They began to speak in languages they had never learned. Now they could teach the gospel to people in other countries.

People heard about what had happened and began gathering in front of the house where Jesus' followers were. Peter went outside to talk to the crowd. He told them that Jesus was the Son of God and that He had gone back to heaven. Peter told the people that God's Spirit had come to them.

Three thousand people believed what Peter told them. They confessed their sins. Peter baptized the new believers.

Paul Meets Jesus (Acts 9:1-19)

Jesus' followers were sharing the good news of Jesus' resurrection with anyone who would listen. More and more people believed on Jesus, and they too shared the good news with even more people.

A man named Paul (also called Saul) was unhappy about all the new believers. Paul even watched as a man named Stephen was stoned to death for believing in Jesus. Paul traveled all over the city looking for believers to put in jail.

One day Paul was on his way to Damascus to find believers and punish them. Suddenly a bright light shone down from heaven and a voice spoke, "Saul, Saul, why do you persecute Me?"

"Persecute" means to treat someone very badly. When Paul was punishing people for being Christians, he was really punishing Jesus.

"Who are you?" Paul asked, falling to his knees.

"I am Jesus, the One you are persecuting," the voice answered.

Jesus told Paul to get up and go to the city, and he would be told what to do. Paul was blind when he got up. Paul's friends had to lead him to a house in the city.

God told a man named Ananias to go see Paul. Ananias was afraid. He'd heard about the things Paul had done to believers.

God told Ananias, "I have chosen Paul to go and tell others about me."

Ananias obeyed God and went to the house where Paul was. He put his hands on Paul's head, and Paul could see again!

Paul is Rescued (Acts 9:20-26)

Now that Paul believed on Jesus, he began preaching about Jesus with the same enthusiasm he had when he was punishing believers. Now he proclaimed, "Jesus was the perfect Son of God."

Some of the people who had liked Paul before now thought of him as an enemy. They wanted to kill him.

Paul's new friends heard about the plot to kill Paul. In the middle of the night, they hid Paul in a basket. Then they lowered him down through a hole in the city wall. Paul was safe! He went to Jerusalem to be with other believers there.

Peter in Jail (Acts 12:1-19)

King Herod Agrippa didn't like the believers. He arrested them and he even had some of them killed. Herod threw Peter into prison for preaching about Jesus. He planned to have Peter killed later. But God wasn't done using Peter to spread the gospel. One night Peter was asleep when an angel appeared to him. "Quick, get up," the angel told Peter.

The chains binding him fell off, and Peter got up.

"Wrap your cloak around yourself and follow me," the angel told Peter.

Peter followed the angel out of the locked prison gates and out onto the street. Then the angel disappeared.

Peter went to a house where many believers were gathered together praying. The servant girl told the believers that Peter was at the door, but no one believed her. Peter had to knock on the door again! Everyone was amazed that Peter was free!

❂ Prayer Pocket Craft ❂

Make It!

The believers were praying for Peter's release, but they were still surprised when it happened! We need to remember to pray everyday — and believe that God will answer. Here is an easy craft to remind you to pray.

▶ You Need:

❀ Old pair of jeans or other pants that are ready to be thrown out (ask for permission)

❀ Fabric paint in your favorite colors

❀ Piece of paper cut into strips

❀ Thumb tacks

❀ Pen or pencil

My Prayer Pocket

▶ To Do:

❀ Cut a back pocket off of the jeans. Cut the bottom piece that it is sewn to. Cut around the outside of the pocket through both layers of material. You should have a pouch when you are done.

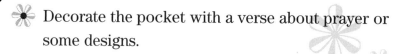

- Decorate the pocket with a verse about prayer or some designs.

- Allow the pocket to dry.

- Put the prayer pocket near your bed.

- Write your prayer requests on slips of paper and put them into the pocket.

- At night or in the morning, take out the slips and pray for those prayer requests. Then put them back in the pocket so that you can pray for them again.

Optional: Make a second prayer pocket for answered prayer requests. For example, if you are praying for a sick friend, move the prayer request slip to the answered prayer pocket when your friend gets well.

Paul's Missionary Trips

Paul went on three mission trips. Barnabas was his partner on the first trip. Silas went with him on the second and third trips. During these mission trips, Paul told many people about Jesus. Some people believed the gospel message and some didn't.

Do you remember when Katie and Sarah's dad told them about the young man who fell asleep in church and fell out the third story window? That happened during a missionary trip. All the believers in a town called Troas

gathered in an upstairs room of a house to hear Paul. Paul talked for a long time because he was leaving the next day. It was late at night, and a young man named Eutychus was sitting in the window. He fell asleep and fell out the third story window to the ground! Everyone rushed outside, but it was too late; Eutychus was dead. Paul took Eutychus into his arms, and Eutychus was alive again. Everyone went back into the house and rejoiced. They ate and then Paul talked until morning. This time Eutychus stayed awake!

How do you think Eutychus might have felt after Paul brought him back to life?

_____

_____

Paul is Arrested (Acts 21:27-40)

Paul preached every chance he got. His enemies put him in prison. Paul was going to be taken to Rome to be tried for telling people about Jesus.

Once in Rome, Paul was kept prisoner in a house, but even then he told people about Jesus. No matter what happened to Paul, he kept talking about Jesus.

Paul wrote many letters to friends and new churches. He even wrote some of them while he was in prison! Many of these letters are included in the Bible.

Make It!

✿ Mailbox Craft ✿

Paul wrote letters to his friends and to new churches. Store your own letters in this fun mailbox.

▶ You Need:

- Empty cereal box

- Scissors

- Wrapping paper or paper grocery sack large enough to cover the box

- Paint, markers, or pictures for decorating the box

- Paper fastener

- Tape

- Glue

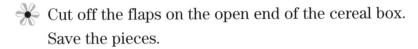

▶ To Do:

✳ Cut off the flaps on the open end of the cereal box. Save the pieces.

✳ Have a parent help you wrap the box with the paper.

✳ Decorate however you wish.

✳ Use the pieces you cut off to make a flag for your mailbox. Use one piece for the straight part. Cut a small triangle out of the other part and tape them together as shown in the illustration.

✳ Use the scissors (have a parent help you) to make a small hole near the bottom of the flag. Make another hole in your mailbox where you want to attach it. Use the paper fastener to attach the flag to the box.

✳ Use the mailbox for letters or school papers. Put the flag up when there are papers in your mailbox.

You've Got Mail

Chapter 9

Katie and Sarah ran through the door from school. "We're home," Katie called.

"There's some mail for you on the table," Mom said.

Katie and Sarah ran over to the table.

"Letters from Grandma!" they shouted.

Letters from Grandma were always fun. She not only wrote a letter, but she always included pictures or comics that she thought they'd like.

"It's greeting cards this time," Sarah said as she pulled hers out.

"Cool," Katie said opening hers. They both sat down to read their mail.

The Epistles

The Epistles were letters written either to churches or to specific Christians. Sometimes the letters were written to correct a problem, while others offered encouragement. Some gave advice about running a church.

Romans

Paul wrote this book to the church in Rome. The Christians in Rome were treated very badly for their faith. Sometimes they hid in long tunnels and rooms under the city. The letter told them that everyone is a sinner and needs a Savior. It told them that when they had Jesus as their Savior they would have eternal life in heaven with God. Paul reminded the Christians that they should try to please God by obeying him.

Read this important message from Romans using the speedometer code below.

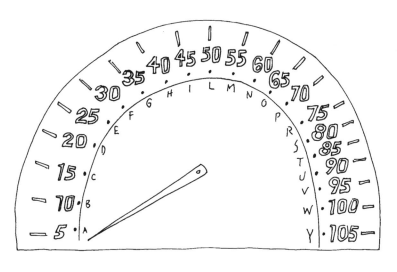

___ ___ ___   ___ ___ ___ ___   ___ ___   ___ ___ ___
85 40 25   35 45 30 85   65 30   35 65 20

___ ___   ___ ___ ___ ___ ___ ___ ___   ___ ___ ___ ___.
45 80   25 85 25 75 60 5 50   50 45 30 25

— Romans 6:23

1&2 Corinthians
Paul wrote these two books to the church in Corinth. Corinth was an important city in Greece.

The Christians in Corinth had problems. They became angry with each other easily and argued frequently. Paul wrote these letters to teach them how to get along. He reminded them that the church is made up of all sorts of people. Everyone has different talents they can use to help the church.

Paul told the people to help others in need. He warned them not to listen to false teachers who would try to turn them away from Jesus.

1 Corinthians 13 is known as the "love chapter" because it tells us very clearly what love is and isn't. Hold the message below up to a mirror to read this important message from 1 Corinthians.

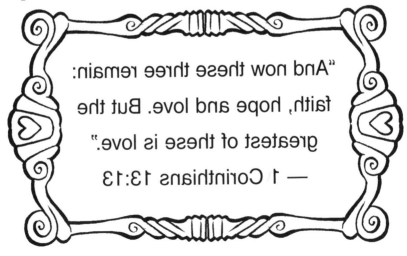

"And now these three remain: faith, hope and love. But the greatest of these is love."
— 1 Corinthians 13:13

Galatians

Paul wrote this letter to the churches in Galatia. Paul wrote the letter to remind them that they were saved by faith in Jesus, not by anything they could do. He told them that the Holy Spirit would help them to do right, and when they let God's Spirit work in them, other people would see God's fruit (good characteristics) in them.

Read Galatians 5:22-23. These verses list nine fruits of the Spirit that will be in everyone who allows God's Spirit to work in them. Write the nine characteristics on the fruit below.

Ephesians
Paul wrote this letter to the church at Ephesus. Ephesus was at the crossroads of important trade routes during that time. Many people in Ephesus worshipped the false goddess Diana. Paul wrote the letter to remind the people that they were saved by God's grace. He wanted them to live in ways that please God. Paul told the Ephesians that they have special spiritual armor to help them. Read Ephesians 6:10-18 to match the spiritual armor that Paul mentions with the pieces below.

Philippians
Paul wrote this letter to the church at Philippi to thank the Christians at Philippi for money they had sent him and for their encouragement. Even though Paul was in jail when he wrote this letter, he told the Christians to pray and rejoice and be thankful no matter what happened.

Colossians

Paul wrote this letter to the church at Colossae, a market town. False teachers were teaching the people that they should worship angels and keep Jewish ceremonies. Paul told the Christians that they should know who Jesus is and worship only Him. He reminded them to live holy lives and to do their best in everything as though they were doing it for the Lord. Follow the maze below to learn for yourself.

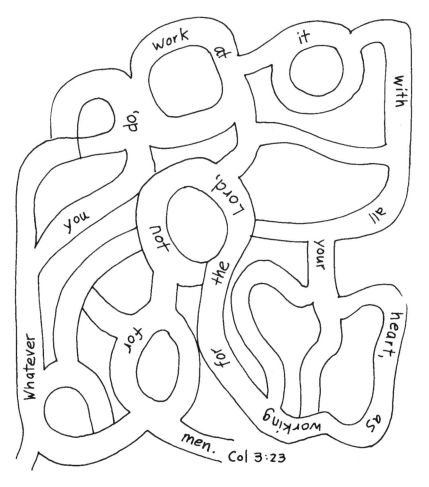

Col 3:23

1&2 Thessalonians

Paul wrote these two letters to the church at Thessalonica. Thessalonica was a busy seaport. It was at the junction of two main roads. Paul wrote these letters to tell the church that Jesus would come again one day. Some Christians decided to do nothing but just wait for Christ's return. Paul told them to work hard because no one knows when Christ will come again.

⊙ Falling into Thankfulness ⊙

1 Thessalonians 5:18 says, "Give thanks in all circumstances, for this is God's will for you in Christ Jesus." We set aside Thanksgiving Day each year to give thanks for our blessings. But don't wait until then to have an attitude of gratitude. You can do this project any time of year.

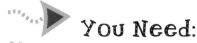 **You Need:**

 Leaf pattern on the following page

 Colored construction paper

 Pen or marker

❋ Scissors

❋ Tape

▶ **To Do:**

❋ Trace the leaf pattern onto the colored paper and cut out. Make as many leaves as you want.

❋ On each leaf write something for which you are thankful. Be specific. Say, "I'm thankful for ham and pineapple pizza" rather than "I'm thankful for food." Ask family members to write down what they are thankful for also.

I am thankful for my parents

I am thankful for my pets

I am thankful for my coat

I am thankful for my books

I am thankful for my basketball hoop

❋ Find a special place to tape your leaves. See how many you can do altogether. Read them often to remember to give God thanks for the good things he does for us.

1&2 Timothy
Paul wrote these two letters to Timothy, a young man who was in charge of the church at Ephesus. Paul wrote to tell Timothy how to be a good pastor. He told Timothy how to choose good church leaders and how to be a good example in speech, life, love, faith, and purity.

Titus Paul wrote to Titus, a believer who had traveled with Paul on some of his journeys. He worked with the churches in Corinth and Crete. In this letter, Paul tells Titus how to deal with problems in the church at Crete. Paul instructed Titus how to choose good church leaders.

Philemon Paul wrote this letter to Philemon, a friend in Colossae. Philemon's slave, Onesimus, had run away. Onesimus met Paul and became a Christian. Paul asked Philemon to take Onesimus back and not to punish him. He told Philemon that Onesimus was a brother in Christ now.

Hebrews This letter was written to Jews who believed in Jesus. Hebrews was written to say that Jesus is greater than the prophets, angels, and the high priests before him. It told the believers that Jesus was the everlasting High Priest. Hebrews talks about Old Testament characters who had strong faith.

Do You Know? Why are each of the following Old Testament heroes famous? Match the hero with their faithful trait. (*Hint:* Read Hebrews 11—it will help!)

1. By faith _____ offered a better sacrifice than Cain did.

2. By faith _____ built an ark to save his family.

3. By faith _____ offered Isaac as a sacrifice when God tested him.

4. By faith _____'s parents hid him for three months after he was born.

5. By faith _____ welcomed the spies.

Hero:

Noah

Abel

Rahab

Abraham

Moses

James

James wrote to believers who were scattered throughout many countries. He told them how to face troubles in their Christian life. He also shared that they should live out their faith by doing good things for others. They should control their tongues and be patient in hard times.

1 & 2 Peter

Peter knew that some Christians were suffering because they believed in Jesus. Peter reminded them that they had a new life in Christ and that they were to be holy and obey God. He instructed them to watch out for people who taught things that weren't true and reminded them that Jesus would come back some day.

1, 2, & 3 John

John, a disciple of Jesus, wrote these three short letters. They were probably passed from church to church. Third John was written to John's friend Gaius. John wanted to remind the church that they had eternal life in Jesus. He wanted them to live for Jesus and not listen to false teachers.

Jude

This letter, written by Jude, warns churches about the dangers of false teachers. There are only 25 verses in the whole book of Jude!

There is only one book of the Bible left, but it's a very important book. It tells us about heaven.

Try this:

These books you've just read about were all letters that taught people about Jesus. Try writing a letter of your own to tell someone about Jesus.

Dear _____

_____

_____

_____

Your friend, _____

Amazing Endings
and
New Beginnings

Chapter 10

Tales from
Sarah
& Katie

Katie and Sarah were very sad. Their grandfather had died and they had just returned from his funeral. A lot of relatives they didn't know had been there. They all talked about Grandpa. Then there had been a meal at the church. Now Katie and Sarah were getting ready for bed.

Katie and Sarah's older brother Jesse came into the room along with their older sister Jenni. Their mom and dad joined them as they talked about Grandpa.

"I'm sad," Katie said. "I miss Grandpa."

"Me, too," Sarah said. "Thanksgiving and Christmas won't be the same without him."

"No, it won't be the same," Dad said.

"Are you sad too, Dad?" Jesse asked.

"I'm sad because I miss Grandpa. But at the same time I'm happy because I know he's in heaven, and that's the best place to be," Dad answered.

"How do you know what heaven is like?" Sarah asked.

"The Bible tells us about heaven. It also tells us about a new heaven and a new earth," Dad said. "Let me get my Bible, and I'll tell you what it says."

Revelation
Revelation tells about things to come, so it's called a book of prophecy. John, a disciple of Jesus, wrote the book of Revelation. The book of Revelation starts with messages to seven churches. Each church was told about the things they were doing right and the things they were doing wrong.

John's Visions

John saw a vision of heaven and the throne of God. John also describes punishments that will happen in the future to people who don't believe in Jesus.

A New Beginning

At the end of Revelation, John describes a vision of a new heaven and a new earth. The streets are paved with gold and the gates are made of precious pearls. The foundation and the walls are made of precious stones. God will live with His people there, and everyone will always be happy. Amazing!

Jesus' promise

The Bible ends with a very special promise.

Do You Know? What was Jesus' promise?

Use the code below to read Jesus' words. Jesus

promised to come again and to bring rewards with Him to give to everyone according to what they had done.

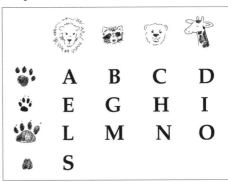

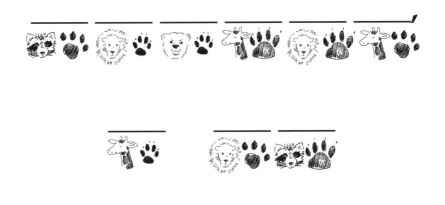

— Revelation 22:12

We've gone all the way through the Bible, but don't stop now. Take time to read the Bible for yourself a little bit every day!

Answers

❋ Just for Me! ❋

Page 15-16: God Creates the World Word Scrabble

Answers: 1. Day and night; 2. Sea and sky;

3. Land, plants, and trees; 4. Sun, moon, and stars;

5. Birds and fish; 6. Animals and man; 7. God rested

Page 19: Do You Know? Matching Game

Answers: Lion-Cub; Cat-Kitten; Horse-Foal; Kangaroo-Joey;

Alligator-Hatchling; Pig-Piglet

Page 25: Do You Know? Hidden Word

Answer: Faith

Page 27: Forgiving Others Word Puzzle

Answer: *Forgive as the Lord forgave you.* — Colossians 3:12

Page 34-35: Do You Know? Word Puzzle

Answer: *Strike the rock, and water will come out of it for the people to drink.* — Exodus 17:6.

Page 40: Joshua's Words

Answer: *The Lord is with us. Do not be afraid.*
— Numbers 14:9

Page 44: Do You Know? Joshua's Message

Answer: *Choose for yourselves this day whom you will serve.* — Joshua 24:15

Page 54: Do You Know? God Rejects Saul

Answer: *To obey is better than sacrifice.* — 1 Samuel 15:22

Page 56: David Maze

Page 60: Solomon is Wise

Answer: A wise heart (1 Kings 3:12)

Page 65-66: Word Bank

Answer: 1. Moses; 2. Samuel; 3. Joshua; 4. Gideon; 5. David; 6. Solomon; 7. Joash

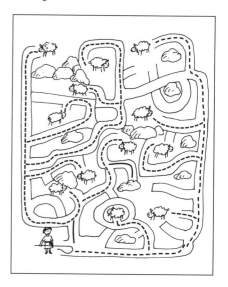

Page 78: Do You Know? Proverbs Word Code

Answer: *A gentle answer turns away wrath.* — Proverbs 15:1

Page 86: God's Promise

Answer: *For I know the plans I have for you...plans to give you hope and a future.* — Jeremiah 29:11

Page 98: Do You Know? Habakkuk's Message

Answer: *I will be joyful in God my Savior.* — Habakkuk 3:18

Page 104: Do You Know? Jesus' Birth

Answer: John (Luke 1:60)

✳ Just for Me! ✳

Page 135: Romans speedometer code

Answer: *The gift of God is eternal life.* — Romans 6:23

Page 136: 1&2 Corinthians Mirror Message

Answer: *And now these three remain: faith, hope and love. But the greatest of these is love.* — 1 Corinthians 13:13

Page 137: Fruits of the Spirit

Answer: Love, joy, peace, patience, kindness, goodness, faithfulness, gentleness, self-control

Page 138: Armor of God

Answer: Belt of truth, breastplate of righteousness, shoes of readiness, shield of faith, helmet of salvation, sword of the Spirit

Page 139: Working for the Lord Maze

Answer: *Whatever you do, work at it with all your heart, as working for the Lord, not for men.* — Colossians 3:23

Page 143: Do You Know? Old Testament Heroes

Answers: 1. Abel; 2. Noah; 3. Abraham; 4. Moses; 5. Rahab

Page 148: Jesus' Promise

Answer: *Behold, I am coming soon!* — Revelation 22:12